The Other Woman

Toby Olson

The Other Woman

—a brief memoir

Shearsman Books

Published in the United Kingdom in 2015 by
Shearsman Books
50 Westons Hill Drive
Emersons Green
Bristol
BS16 7DF

www.shearsman.com

ISBN 978-1-84861-427-7

ACKNOWLEDGEMENT
This memoir first appeared, in a slightly different form,
in *Gold Handcuffs Review*.

Cover
'Cerulean Blue, Light to Dark'
by David von Schlegell.

With thanks to Mark von Schlegell
and Susan Howe.

Contents

In memory of my dear wife Miriam,
lover and friend

this week

This week, for most of it at least, I am her father. Though things can change. I can be her brother, husband or uncle, even – and this touches me deeply – "My Good Friend." But for now it's "My Father," and that spoken in an oddly formal way. "Be careful, My Father," as I descend the stairs, or "Thank you, My Father," as I take hold of her hands and pull her slowly to her feet. Maybe it's just "My Father," an announcement spoken through a wistful smile as I walk backward, guiding her toward the bathroom.

What can it mean, this transaction between us that her words initiate? I am nothing like her father, though both of us are approaching his age now, the age at which he died. In the Alzheimer's Care Givers Group, most probably because of my overwrought enthusiasm, it's suggested that it may be a religious matter, this My Father, referring to the one in heaven or his representative. After all I do tend to dress all in black these days, though I wear no priest's collar. This response is funny and very kind in its engagement with what may well be my foolishness.

Her father was an immigrant from somewhere in Russia. He came here with nothing but a few relatives and managed to work his way into the ownership of a modest paint store on Third Avenue in Manhattan. He was a simple man, his few foibles suffered kindly by his young wife and four daughters. There are three daughters now, and two of them call on occasion, but no longer visit. They used to speak with Miriam, but now when I hold the phone to her ear she says nothing at all to them, though she seems to listen with some intensity. I don't know if there is a reason.

A few years ago, when my niece Sara was visiting here in Truro, she noticed that Miriam, though already quite inarticulate by then, would read out the road signs – yield, school zone, slow – deaf child – as we approached them. It took me a while to remember that when she was just a little girl she would ride in her father's truck from the Bronx to his paint store in Manhattan in the early morning. Maybe she was six years old? And she'd read the signs – Bruckner Boulevard, Triborough Bridge, East End Avenue – much to her father's delight. He'd urge her on.

In Miriam's family, there seemed little room for conversation or anger. Four young girls after all, a father who worked from dawn to dusk six days a week, and a mother who busied herself with housekeeping and cooking. Of the four girls, Miriam was the only one who learned to cook at her mother's elbow. And she learned well. There are manila folders full of scraps of paper on which recipes are written. They contain phrases like "cover or a little more than cover," "heat until all is ready," "chop fish to the proper consistency," and these words in their comedy made for a powerful connection between mother and daughter.

At times I overburden Miriam with my anxiety and shenanigans, and she gets angry. But her anger seems half-hearted, her look that of a stern librarian, but without clear object. She's looking at me, sort of, her eyes vacant as if there is nothing understood behind or in front of them. "I'm sorry," she says, out of nowhere, and I might reply, "Sorry for what?" but I don't do so, knowing she will have no answer. We are both, after all, sorry: sorry that life has taken this turn, sorry for ourselves, even sorry for each other from time to time. Well, I am. I can't really be sure about her.

"Who am I?" I ask this frequently as I enter a room and note her puzzled expression or approach the bed and pull back the covers. And her answer can be, often has been, "Which one are you?"

"There's more than one of us?" I ask.

"Well, yes," she might say, almost articulate. "There's you, Toby, and the other guy."

"I'm the middle one," I say. "That Toby."

A brief smile then and we fall into sleep beside each other, never touching, though I awaken with her hand on my back, her knee pressed against my thigh, tentative, in the way of virginal lovers examining. In our earlier years, we slept close together, always entangled.

In the Care Givers Group, Lee's wife of so many years has passed away, or died, or been released from her suffering, releasing Lee as well. It all depends on who you are and how you look at things. Lee continues to come to our meetings, though his reason for being there is now absent. For the sake of a kind of continuity. He speaks up on occasion, but now his talk is of loss and history. He is mostly silent. A woman in the group speaks of the problems she's having with her husband and his driving. He won't give up his license or the keys. "Why don't you just take them?" one of the men asks, but she can't do that. He won't let her. The women here seem to have much more difficulty with their demented spouses than do the men. Something about gender that is more complex than I can understand.

Here in Truro there are no stores open in the winter, so I drive to Provincetown to buy a condolence card. And for the first time in my life, instead of one I buy two. One for Lee and one for the next.

"My Father," Miriam says, her eyes bright and somewhat vacant, and I want to hear the questions following: "My father, are you lonely?" My father, can I help you?" "Bless you, My Father."

She's in the house, beautiful brown eyes staring at nothing, and I'm here in my study, writing this, my story.

It feels like cheating.

saints

Some think of me as a saint. There are those who have said as much. All of them have been women. And I have demurred, very much as a saint might, eyes lowered in humility.

What would it be like to be married to a saint, at least to sleep with one? I can see it in their eyes and know the advantages that I have. *And after the loving and the tenderness and the sacred touch, to be cared for as he cares for her: the washing, the massages, his lips upon my wasted body.* There are no massages. Her body is too tender for that, though from time to time I do rub her feet. And the washing is done by the home health care aid, the cheerful and beautiful Pat, another who has granted me that saintly designation. I had become awkward in the bathing, at times enraged in ways saints might find shameful. In ways *she* found shameful, beautiful brown eyes focused in mine. I was seared and looked away.

When Mother Teresa arrived in heaven she was not yet a saint, but this was heaven, where the future is known as well as all details of the past, and Peter placed a small saint's halo above the good mother's head. Then she was allowed entrance into paradise.

One day, while walking around in the clouds, the soon to be a Saint Teresa spied a gathering of women a short distance away, and at the center of the group, attended by the others, stood Princess Diana, and floating above her head was a halo at least four times the size of the one Teresa sported. In consequence, she approached and then spoke.

"Look here, young lady, I'm Mother Teresa. I have tended extensively to the poor and diseased in the black holes of Calcutta. I have been awarded the Nobel Prize. I will soon be a saint. How is it then that you, nothing more than a bit of royalty, should be topped by a halo four times the size of mine? Please explain yourself."

The young lady looked down at the aged mother, smiled, then spoke.

"This is no halo, my dear, this is a steering wheel!"

All the attendant ladies laughed then, raucously. Mother Teresa learned a lesson in humility.

And we might learn a lesson too, about saints and saintliness. The good mother, after all, objected to both birth control and abortion, and this while tended to those victimized by, according to her saintly rules, the absence of both.

I am not a saint, though I confess to some satisfaction in being thought of as such. And in the lives of the saints, there is much pain delivered – arrows, whips, fire – for purification or cleansing. And I have feelings about that, romance of my frustration, depression, night terrors. I weep at the oddest times, staring at a flower on a greeting card, the strains of sentimental music. There are feelings in here, somewhere, that I can't quite locate. I am like the Norwegian farmer who loved his wife so much he almost told her. I may have little to be ashamed of, but I am profoundly ashamed. I have not mentioned Miriam's name one time in this rumination.

A woman is telling a story, about her mother and breathing. Her mother, now institutionalized, can't find a place for her body. She gulps air, then stops, then shifts painfully into another position, and for a while she can breath easily. Then the gulping starts again, and the nurse has to turn her. The woman can't help with this turning. She feels guilty. The end is near. Silence creeps into the room. Someone is quietly weeping.

Another woman in the Alzheimer's Care Givers Group was visited by an angel. She had felt "at loose ends," quoted here since in her mouth the words seemed quite literal: ends at the perimeter within which one might feel control; they had come loose, and now the guarding perimeter itself was falling away. It was nothing specific, she said, nothing to do, at least visually, but care for her husband and keep a good house, details she could only handle in a perfunctory fashion.

"Is there nothing I can do?" the Visiting Angel asked her.

"Well," she said, there's the refrigerator. "I know it's in disorder, though it's out of sight, and that bothers me, that out of control feeling?"

So the Angel spent her time in washing and ordering and throwing things away, and when she was finished the refrigerator was clean and gleaming.

"There," she said.

And the woman reported that the cleaning was a very powerful thing indeed. It was as if her insides had been reordered, and though they, like the bowels of the refrigerator, were out of sight, they made it possible to arrange such order on the outside as well. "Or at least I could feel okay when disorder took over, however briefly. I could tend to my husband without care. I was able to focus my attention exclusively upon him."

Visiting Angels and Saints. A world beyond the ordinary. Everyone in the group lives there, each in his or her way. We are close to the outposts of human existence, those places where people fall apart, however slowly, before going to whatever existence we, in our various beliefs, might send them. Earth to earth, ashes to ashes, heaven or some other great beyond, a mingling with the chemicals of existence. Who can say? We each say.

And in the meantime we hold to fragments, to the smile or even the frown that seemed to be personal, exclusively for us. There is nothing else to do, lest we put them away and forget them, which for us is impossible.

her smile

And yet her smile, empty of guile, not reminiscent of but exactly the same as it always has been. Trusting and delighted, welcoming, those qualities all the more apparent now that so much else has faded into a background of silhouettes. My heart is broken. By that smile I have charted my course. Once upon a time. Gone now. There are bits of food along the gum line. She no longer brushes her teeth, and I am the poor, shadow actor standing behind her whose attempts to negotiate the task are failures. Once upon a time. *Little little little little little little.* Her finger points at her tightly closed fist. Is there something there? Something for me there? Much like a game we used to play, a romantic toying. "I have something to show you here. Come here and see it." Then I would grab and pull her down to the chair, couch, bed. Give her a kiss. "Give me a kiss," I say. *Little little little little little little.*

And then, for the first time since winter, I push her out onto the deck, into the sun, in her wheelchair. It's warm enough, though I spread a large black shawl over her shoulders. Big smile. "Do you like it out here?" "Yess". "It's nice and warm, huh?" "I don't know. " "But you like it, right?" Why do I torture myself this way. She doesn't answer. Then, quite miraculously, a large wild turkey strolls into view, no more than thirty feet away. "Look! A wild turkey!," I whisper. No response. "Do you see it Miriam, a wild turkey, right there!" I point and even touch her cheek to urge her gaze in the right direction. The turkey is pecking at seed below the feeder, looking around, preening. Now Miriam is smiling. She seems to be gazing at the turkey. And the turkey has lifted its head from its flared wing and seems to be gazing at her. But how can we know what a turkey sees?

Beyond the turkey and the wild, aggressive swans in Zurich and the storks in Norway and the Arizona road runner and flamingoes on Bonaire, she is smiling, and I am for that reason smiling too. Smiling with tears in her eyes. Smiling while singing while listening to music, while attempting to sing, while making love and afterward, her smile a miracle of expression. Even smiling in anger when I have, in some small way, done her wrong.

Perhaps the time has come for me to tell the truth. Over the years, I have desired many women and have slept with some. This is a truth I would not tell were I younger. But I'm an old man now, and those who would question my character are, for the most part, long gone. This could have been a breaking point, but it wasn't. She didn't smile when I told her of an escapade. She is a woman of backbone even now, though scoliosis has twisted her spine. She can hardly walk, but with a smile she struggles to do so. I urge her on.

On our first date, when I was a California hick in New York City, a hole in the elbow of my cheap sweater, ridiculous pants, we went to a inexpensive French restaurant that she had chosen, knowing that I was but a poor graduate student. I was twenty-seven, she a few years older and a professional, teaching classes at Columbia University. She guided me into ordering a few nice things from the menu, escargot, veal, and I added a bottle of what I thought was good wine. We ate and talked, and when our meal ended, with crème brulée, and I paid the bill, we went out into a light rain. We had planned on the bus, but she suggested, given the rain, that we take a taxi. It was an awkward moment. I was almost out of money, and I told her this. "Could you lend me a few dollars?" She found this charming. Then she dug in her purse, and when she handed me a twenty dollar bill, she turned her face up to me in the rain. She was smiling, and from that moment on she had me, or I had her.

I sit now in my study, thinking about that time and other times that have passed out of existence, for though the smile is still there, I can no longer be sure of what is behind it. A smile can be a guarding against intimacy, but it can also be an invitation. Am I invited into her mind, her feelings, those inexpressibles? What's next? Can you give me a hint, some message within that message? A smile can be an expression of confidence.

Once at the cusp of our desire and after surgery, we found that the sheet we lay on was soaked with her warm blood. I rested in that sticky wetness, and it was she who rose from the bed and called the doctor. I begrudge her nothing in this ugly and unforgiving life. Though I pity myself, though I turn my old eyes to the bodies of other women, and though I forgive myself readily, her smile is without judgment, only understanding, and I think she can read my mind. The future is the next moment, the significant past but the bed's edge from which I have helped her rise.

I will gather her wasted body in my arms and lower her to the toilet. She will look up at me, and smile.

talk

I imagine or I remember, in a time when I was much younger, uncles and aunts, or the parents of friends or acquaintances, talking about their time together when they were in that time called by most everybody, but for the ones within it, old age. Oh, the ones within it would name it that, but only jokingly, for I know now that they felt young enough, and elderly was experienced as an insult when applied to them.

They spoke quietly and privately, even in the presence of others, and lightly between each other, smiles, nudges, and focused pupils, of aches and pains, of the increasing slowness of their walking, holding hands, ignoring the clucking of passing girls and young couples who thought them cute and lovey-dovey. They would have told them to fuck themselves, but they were more dignified than that, even those in the working class, retired tradesmen and railroad conductors and women secretaries from the Western Electric Company. Talk of changes in medications, urinary urgency, rotator cuff discomfort and back trouble that came upon them even after light work in the garden. They remembered when, and spoke about that when somewhat quizzically. How could it be? I don't feel all that different in my mind.

When Dick Cavett was asked how he felt now that he had entered a certain age, his reply, as I remember, was that he didn't feel like an old man; he felt like a young man who had something wrong with him. This is the way the talk went, and really, it seems to me now, it was love talk, exchanges between two people who had come a long way together and were now savoring what they knew to be the beginning of the ending of that time. They were marking every moment of every change, and they would continue to do so until the very end. I won't have that, and I ache for it.

Little little little little little little. I've asked Miriam about her eye, which is severely blood-shot. "Does it hurt? Do you hurt somewhere? *Little little little little little little.* Her hand presents a closed fist. A remembered gesture from a little game of ours? Or does her finger pointing at that fist suggest something broader, less specific, a thing in some atmosphere? I don't know. I'll never know. I have no one to talk with, and I have aches and pains, am no longer comfortable reading in bed next to her. I know she's staring at me. I doubt that she sees me. For moments yesterday, I was her daughter. "My daughter," she said.

Ten or more years back, near the start of this, we were together in the doctor's waiting room filling out papers, and I found that Miriam was having trouble with her questionnaire. So I suggested that she let me ask her the questions and then I'd write down her answers. The room was crowded, and since we were speaking to each other, listing past conditions and family histories, others in the room were listening to us. And in the course of things, I came to a series of questions about how she felt and asked her the following one.

"Do you experience any pain?"

"Only when it hurts," was her reply, and the room burst into laughter at her answer. I laughed too and looked up at her. She was smiling, but only because of the laughter. She had no idea what was so funny. That's when these feelings regarding talk leading to endings began. That's when I began to find myself feeling increasingly alone.

But you are not alone, people say. You have friends, you have relatives. Everyone is there for you. And this is all correct, but for one very important thing, and it is this that such intimate talk between people in old age is all about. It's a negotiation. It's laying one's cards on the table. It's about the body. It's about sex.

When I was much younger, I wrote a poem containing the phrase "sex is life." Then for a while, looking back on that poem and statement I thought I had been naive and foolish. Now, in old age, I think otherwise.

Please watch my shoulder. Be careful of my ankle. My back can't handle that position. Slowly, slowly. That's it. Exactly there. Careful of my breast. Your tongue tastes of chocolate. No, the index finger. Can you rest on your elbows? Can you lift me a little? Go slowly now, but don't stop. I love you. I mean it. I know, I know. You don't have to say it. I do, I do. It never gets old. It never gets old. It never gets old.

the mornings

Monday

Up at five-thirty. Pills and coffee. Then out to my study, email and the on-line New York Times. Mid-May, and it's raining, the windows fogged and lightly pinged with slanting drops. Even through the quiet rain rush, I can hear the sharp note of a cardinal, twitter of sparrows at the thistle feeder. Miriam is sleeping, and I'm biding my time.

Then it's seven. Pat comes at eight, so I'm back at the bedside, standing above Miriam, who is still sleeping. I can see her breath, tentative, in her back. Wake up. Softly. I'd put the heat on earlier. It's warm now, it's a cold, cold morning. Wake up.

Groggy, as always, as with anyone. "What? I don't…" "What?" I say. "I don't know," she says. A complete sentence. I peel the covers back. Her legs, thin now, below her nightgown hem. And lift her at the knees and turn her, take her hands and sit her up. Then it's walking backward to the stairlift's chair, holding her hands, whereupon she sits. Struggle of the nightgown, then standing again, her two hands in one of mine against grabbing, and pull her diaper down. She sits again, and I lift the diaper away, heavy with urine. Then it's into the bathroom and onto the toilet. She's smiling, looking at me.

From the toilet, after a brief flow of urine, I take her hands and lift her, turn and, once again shuffling backward, lead her to the sink. Then I turn and step back and see her spine and each rib, distinct as in some book, the *Grey's Anatomy* out in my study. Her scapulas, her iliac crest, her coccyx, the slump of her buttocks. She's wasting away, and yet I see her personality in all of it. The way she stands, the way her thighs touch, the stature of her neck. Where we've been and where we are going. All these years, all these years.

It's time to brush her teeth, and I stand at her shoulder once again and look at her face in the mirror, then apply the swallowable toothpaste to the brush. Then I move behind her, and as if my arm grew from her shoulder, I begin a slow and difficult brushing. She doesn't like it. She jerks her head from side to side to get away from it. Toothpaste smears her lips. Rage rises in me. I pause and swallow it. Then she swallows the toothpaste. I provide a chaser of water.

And then with various wet and dry wipes I clean her vagina and anus. There's a little fecal matter there, and I have to take some time with it. And I must say in truth, the time is in part taken because of the intimacy. No sex anymore. But there is this, this touching and cleaning of these most private places: mouth, vagina, and anus. When I look at her face in the mirror, as I wipe her, she's smiling. Pat comes at eight. She'll come again on Wednesday.

Tuesday

On Tuesdays I rise as usual, around five-thirty or close to that. Then it's pills and coffee again and out to the study for email and just a bit of the New York Times. The moments for solitude are shorter, but that's okay. I'll have most of the day for shopping, cleaning, maybe a little reading. It's The Gathering Place day, Miriam's day care, twenty or so miles away.

She rises, I help her rise up, at six-thirty. Then it's the same as Monday, ablutions, then down stairs on her stairlift for coffee and the morning news. She looks at the small TV in the kitchen. I'm not sure she sees it.

We leave at seven-fifteen, after a struggle to get her coat on. I've mastered the wheelchair negotiation. She stands up, shuffles in place turning, and I sneak in from her off side and slip the chair behind her. At the door, always as if it's the first time, and it may actually be that for her, it's "Oh, oh, oh!" as I tilt the chair down the two inches to the front porch. Then it's an easy trip down the ramp and to the wooden walkway, then up on her feet again and a few steps on gravel to the car. Just a little struggle to get her turned and onto the passenger seat. I load the trash in the trunk with the wheelchair and we are off to the dump and day care, a little talk on the way, all of it from me.

At The Gathering Place we're met by Jill or Cindy. Both have big smiles and gentle words for Miriam. And once she sees them, it seems to me she quickens her step and stands more erect. Laughing and nodding, she touches them on the arms or shoulders, and I'm a little angry and a little sad and feeling guilty. I might as well not be there, or anywhere, and so after saying goodbye and receiving no response at all, I turn and head back to the car and drive to Orleans to do some grocery shopping, a roasted chicken, a pound of cod, vegetables, some fruit for cereal, a few lamb chops, her favorite, that I have learned to cook, various other things for her dinners. A candy bar for me.

When I was no more than a child, I read books in order to lose myself in their stories, because they were not my story, the one that had hardly begun then, yet was already a tale of bewilderment. *Kristin Lavransdatter*, *The Sun is my Undoing*, tales of villages and cities in which children grow into adulthood and find themselves disillusioned, or step beyond the fog of nostalgia into the light of a new day. Now I'm an old man, and still I read, these books of mystery and its romance, elegant pathology and refined diction, written mostly by women. It seems to take all the time I have to keep up, as if reading were yet another responsibility.

It was yesterday, Monday, and it was evening. And I hear her now as I drive back from Orleans, a distinct mumbling in many voices, conversations with the self she is trying always to recapture. Then she says my name, distinctly, and I rise and put the book down on the end-table and go in to her.

She had told me, almost forty-five years ago, "If I ever become like that, you must promise to kill me." We were waiting for our flight to be called, and a man sat beside his wife close by, trying in vain to console her. She was clearly bewildered, a well-dressed woman in unmatched colors and fabrics, her makeup applied awkwardly, by him I thought. "And he has dressed her with care," Miriam said. "But it hardly matters."

Does it matter anymore to me? I can't be sure. Or to her for that matter, this lovely woman I have lived with for over forty-five years. Surely something must matter, the touch of her bony shoulder, some *little little* pleasure in the food I prepare. Shopping with only her in mind, that must matter. Being a father, mother, a brother or sister. "My Husband," she says, and for a moment it matters.

Pat pulls into the driveway at eight-thirty. Her red Toyota, cheerful and candy-apple in the bright sun. And efficient, as Pat is. I can see her through the kitchen window. She's on her cell phone, arranging her day I guess. We exchange planting advice and recipes, even the food made from them. She was taken with my eggplant parmesan. I've seen pictures of her garden. Good morning Pat.

I've changed Miriam's diaper, brushed her teeth, then put on a fresh diaper and a T-shirt. She's back in bed, curled up on her protective pad, a large rectangle that's spread over the coverlet. I've tucked her under a lose, old Indian blanket. Her head has slipped from the pillow. It always does. I'd brushed her hair, for no good reason, and now it sticks up in disheveled tufts. She's on her side, knees up, and she seems to be sleeping, but when I lean over I see that her eyes are open. She's waiting. I suspect she is. For Pat. Then she hears her footsteps on the stairs, and she smiles. "Pat's here," I say. "Oh, oh, oh… Yesss," she replies.

It was a long time ago, but I remember clearly the first time I held Miriam in my arms. We were in Aspen, Colorado and were standing on a rock ledge above a twisting gorge through which a narrow river coursed, foam and spray far below. The ledge faced another ledge, no more than two feet away. "Just jump," I said. "You can almost step over!" But she was afraid, shaking a little. I lifted her then, as if in preparation for moving across a threshold, and jumped across the brief space to the other side. Then I lowered her to her feet. From then on, except for the last ten years or so, she's been carrying me.

Through graduate school, through the writing of my first novel and many poems, through emotional disarray, through the death of relatives and friends, through all moments of marital turmoil, through success and failure, through sickness and in health. As a lover, wife and mother, both financially and emotionally: my sister, confidant, and nurse. Now it's my turn.

"Hi Miriam. How are you today?" Pat whispers softly. Miriam turns her head and smiles. I hover, as usually, behind them. "I'm going to give you a shower," Pat says. "I'll wash your hair!" And she casts the cover aside and touches Miriam's legs and turns her, then takes her two hands and lifts her to a sitting position. "Come now," and she slowly pulls her to her feet. Then they shuffle to the stairlift's chair, and Miriam sits down and Pat lifts her again and expertly removes her shirt and pulls down her diaper. Then again they shuffle, into the bathroom. I stay behind, nervous as usual, and hear Pat's soft words of instruction. They seems as much for me as for Miriam, and I go to my bedroom chair and take up my book and read the same paragraph over and over again. It's hard to concentrate. Why can't I just leave them alone? Pat is so clearly kind and efficient, and I feel foolish just sitting here, doing nothing.

Then, in what seems no time at all, they are finished, and Pat is dressing her for the day: shirt, pants and shoes. We talk for a while, about the spring, cooking, and planting, a current TV show, the gardening shed her husband built for her. Easy talk, adult, lucid. Then Pat is gone, and immediately I miss her. There will be others coming tomorrow, Ann, the nurse and Matt, the cleaner, but for now, until Lyndah, the volunteer, comes at eleven, it's just the two of us, breakfast of cereal and coffee. We are alone together, and I am alone. Then Lyndah is there, and I'm off for some "free time," which is anything but free. I do a bit of shopping, then go to play Ping Pong with Lois. Then I go to the ocean beach, stand in the light breeze and watch the surf come in. Gulls drift over the crests, sandpipers rush to the rippling edge, then quickly retreat. It's all beautiful, and it's in my life. What a life.

Today might be a better day. The sun might rise and shine, raindrops still on the long grasses that need cutting and on the two begonias, yellow and red, planted in free time four days ago. There might be a sorcerer or saint upstairs, curing Miriam of this malady that has a name but whose behaviors are beyond clear understanding. I might last for another few weeks without self-pity. Then the phone rings, oddly, at five-thirty in the morning. It's Ruth, Shell's wife. Shell died two years ago.

"Toby. I was so sorry to hear about Miriam."

"Yes. It's been a long haul."

"And you're alone now."

Quickly, it become clear to me. Ruth is suffering from the same thing, Alzheimer's or some other current name, frontal lobe dementia, etc. I haven't spoken to her in a year.

"No, not alone. Miriam is here."

"Oh…" And like Miriam, she can't quite figure how to continue.

A better day, a growing community of the bewildered, does this salve the wounds? How melodramatic.

Perhaps Ruth comes into the house like some glib reporter at a tragedy.

"How does it *feel* to have lost your wife?"

"Routine," I answer.

"But surely… But how can you say such a thing? I'll tell Shell about it. I'll tell Morris." Both of them are dead.

There was lipstick smeared on her mouth, and food particles, and the bodice of her dress was soiled the last time I saw her. She was in that transition period, living alone, but in a minimum care facility. No one, really, was looking after her, washing her face, dressing her, brushing her teeth. There are times when one can do these things for the self. Only, one forgets. That's the beginning. On the phone, with the doctor's office yesterday, I forgot my birth date.

Nurse Ann comes at eight-thirty and takes my blood pressure, both right and left arms. My PA has asked for this, that I phone it in. The systolic was into the one sixties the last time I saw her. Now, for two weeks in a row, it's normal again. No reason that anyone can figure out, least of all me. Then Ann takes Miriam's BP and pulse, listens to her chest and back. Everything, as usual, is normal. It's the way with the progress of this disease, vital signs are no indicator. And measures her arm. She's lost another centimeter, about one a month now. Soon she'll have no more to lose, only skin and bone. She's smiling all the time that Ann is here. She tells her, "You're sooo beautiful!" Ann lingers. Why not? Talks about flowers and planting, thoughts for a few vegetables, grandchildren coming down for the weekend. She holds Miriam's cheeks and kisses her on the forehead before leaving. Miriam is still smiling "Bye, Bye. See you in a week." Then she's out the door. Matt will come to do the cleaning at eleven. We've got almost two hours, for breakfast.

Cereal with plenty of fruit, berries and banana. This morning Miriam can't get started. She sips at her coffee, holds it in both hands and won't put the cup down. I try to leave her to it, but after fifteen minutes, the cereal turning to mush, I can no longer bear it.

I take the cup from her hands, slowly pry her fingers away, rage rising once again in me. Miriam has the grabbies. Anything she gets hold of, my shirt while I am dressing her, a spoon, the inside of a sleeve, a pencil, my wrist, my pant leg, a finger. I breathe deeply and put the cup down. Then I run my fingers over her hand to sooth her. To sooth myself. After that I dip the spoon into the cereal and fruit and feed it to her. Often, I have to feed her the whole bowl, but this morning, a good morning, two spoons seem to prime the pump. She takes the spoon in her fingers and continues eating. I sit back and watch her, delighted with her behavior. These days, I'm not hard to please.

A knock on the door. "Hello," then the door opens. It's Matt, his familiar entrance. Matt cleans for the Visiting Nurses Association, In Home Hospice Care, and Medicare covers this. Good for us, though I'd have to bring someone in anyway. I can't seem to keep up. I remember my mother's place. Dust and dirt everywhere. As we get older, vision and enthusiasm begins to wane. We don't see the dirt, and on the positive side, we don't see our faces and bodies so clearly in the mirror. Wrinkles seem to fade away. We're forever young. Miriam is close to eighty now. I'm seventy-five. Matt will work on the kitchen today, his couple of hours once a week. The cereal is gone, and I help Miriam into her wheelchair and roll her out onto the deck. We'll sit in the sun, vague hum of Matt's vacuum in the background.

It's spring, and the birds are singing. The turkey's back, seen vaguely through bushes in the distance. Bobwhites scurry across the yard, their pecking below the feeder interrupted by our presence. A few high clouds and a warm, gently breeze. Miriam wears a hat, and I sit beside her in one of the lounge chairs. I have a book at hand but am not reading it.

"Do you hear the towhee?" He's kicking around in winter's leaves. There's no response. "Beautiful out here." I speak a little louder. *Little little little little little little.* What can it mean? Miriam turns her head slightly toward me and smiles. Her littles are without their usual urgency. I see her eyes closing under the brim of her hat. I pick up the book, another mystery, and soon my chin has fallen to my chest. A little little nap. It's almost noon, and we are at peace for awhile. Sleeping.

Friday

Friday is the same as Tuesday. I drive Miriam to the Gathering Place. The busses are already there, so I help her into her wheelchair and roll her to the entrance. As always, she's greeted with smiles and light laughter. I say goodbye and kiss her on the cheek. She's not interested. She's all there now and I'm in the disappeared past. Then I drive to Orleans for shopping. Tonight, as usual on Friday, it will be baked cod and fried baby spinach. Easy for Miriam to negotiate this meal, though I may well be feeding it to her anyway. There's some pleasure in that.

Then it's off to Lois's place again, and some Ping Pong, Lois without husband and dog now, and she seems pleased to see me, but this pleasure doesn't soften her competitiveness. She's a wicked player, and I'm lucky to get a game or two. A sweet and valiant woman, who fights constantly to keep her home and self together. Biking, kayaking, speed walking, Pilates, always there's music, and of course this table tennis. We're free of all thought for an hour or more. Her husband, my wife. Bruce and Miriam. We're kindred spirits. I kiss her at the door, then it's back home again and this writing.

When I was a child, my mother used to rearrange the furniture once every couple of weeks. The couch went here, the tables and chairs to a new location, even the few pictures were rehung. She did it to renew her self, to start over in a new place, that was in fact the same old place.

I think it was Steve Martin, his joke about language. The French are amazing, he said, they have a different word for everything. This may be true of course, but when one reaches a certain age or condition, in France, the U.S. or any place, words fall away, are lost or come unstuck from their referents. *Little little little*, the adjective followed by no noun. Fragments of a place then, or presence, "I need something... What does that thing...? I don't have..." As one wastes away, the nose becomes more prominent. And a woman on her back, looked down upon, this woman, Miriam, loses her wrinkles to gravity. Her face becomes young again, her eyes a deeper brown. But I can no longer see that healthy self in herself, but for in photographs, dead things. Those early years, evocative as idea in the memory, are without flesh now; there's no place to park this body of mine, or Miriam's body, but in the imagination. Never a real place. We are both without anchor in our common past. In the beginning? I can't locate that. It's *little little little*, so little as to be almost completely gone away.

Near my house, about a mile's walk away, the North Truro Air force Station, product of the cold war from the fifties into the eighties, lays waste, though it's in the slow process of regeneration to be reborn as, among other things, an art center. The old, weed-choked ball field is still there, as is the NCO Club where airmen as well as locals congregated in good fellowship. And down a blacktop road, reduced to one lane by encroaching weeds, one comes to the Family Housing complex, a gathering of small ranch style structures on slightly twisting streets where once were sidewalks, flower beds, a bus stop kiosk, and a small park. I was there years ago, dropping off an airman who found himself stranded at the golf course. Arriving at his house, I felt as if I had been translated into the Midwest, into a suburban landscape in which tricycles and mothers in house dresses and benign dogs and cats exchanged smiles in play. I'd been there before, in my own growing up, in suburban Illinois, in California and Arizona. The enclave had no business being here on Cape Cod, and yet here it was, a piece of suburban America, perhaps this country's unique contribution to world architecture, even more ubiquitous than Ben Franklin's row houses.

And so I walk those suburban streets now in the early morning. A light breeze blows in waist high weeds at abandoned house sides. What remains of the sidewalks is cracked and grass-choked, and *Warning – Asbestos* is written in faded red on the boarded up windows. The structures, all twenty-five or so houses, seem sound, but squirrels and the occasional fox are the only inhabitants. Early sun glints in places on shingled roofs. Everything on the surface is still, but in rooms seen through dirt-stained windows mold grows on walls, floors and remaining doors. Decay has set in and in time will devour everything. There is no saving this place. I see my body reflected in a cracked pane, an old man, slightly bent over as he stares through. There is decay here as well, time eating away at flesh and at memory. There is no hope for me as there is none for this by-passed village. Goodbye old friends. Then I rise up again, erect for the time being, and head back home to Miriam.

Saturday

If I speak very softly as I stand over her. If I bend down and speak gently into her cheek to whisper her awake. Her eyes open, and I pull back the coverlet and slowly tug up her nightgown to reveal her diaper. It's time for the suppository, and after lifting the diaper's edge, I search with my index finger for her anus. There it is, and I carefully push the small, gelatinous object against her sphincter, still whispering. "It's okay." The ring of her anus gives in with slight pressure, and I push for entrance and insertion, up to the second knuckle of my index finger. When I withdraw, my finger is moist and slightly scented. She turns her head on the pillow and smiles up at me. This is love.

A few weeks before, Miriam was rushed to the hospital from The Gathering Place with large clots of rectal bleeding. I had returned to the place for the Tuesday meeting of the Alzheimer's Discussion Group, and it was there that I learned that Miriam was now in Hyannis. She was there for two nights, then the bleeding stopped and I took her home. I had not allowed any invasive procedures, so the doctor's diagnosis of diverticulosis was only a guess. She prescribed a medication to sooth her bowels and a teaspoon of mineral oil twice a day.

For months Miriam had been suffering from con-stipation, evidenced by a lack of bowel movements but no discernible pain or hardening of the abdomen, and the nurse and I had administered many enemas, only a few of them successful. Though she grew increasingly tired as the days passed and spent a good deal of time sleeping, there were no other symptoms. I now suspect that the enemas, possibly too vigorously applied, had caused a tear in the colon wall. The doctor said that wasn't true.

Now it's suppositories once a week, on Saturday, and while Miriam rests for an hour, I walk down the paths and check the progress of the blueberries. There are thick patches of them everywhere, an early spring morning and overcast. A beautiful morning with no sun glint, and all the burgeoning green is vivid, various yellow wild flowers as punctuation. The berries are coming along, but it's early and they're not yet blue. It's six o'clock and quiet, but for the rustle of a towhee in fallen winter leaves, a few sparrows chirping in scrub oak. I'm tired after restless sleep, but I feel a touch of pleasure or something akin to that. She seemed at peace when I left her there in the bed. We are together in this.

I go in and upstairs and spread the absorbent mats on the floor. One at bed side, one at the stairlift's chair, one at the toilet. This is routine. This is life now. I cast the cover back, turn her, and lift her to her feet. Then we move slowly to the chair and I remove her nightgown, then slip her diaper to the floor and carefully lift her feet free so as not to soil them with feces. I wipe her with a cloth pad, then guide her into the bathroom and over to the toilet, where she sits placidly while I make the bed and order her clothing for the day. When I enter the bathroom again I can smell it. Triumph. There's a smile on her face.

It's these small successes that become large successes as the days go by. To defecate. To speak an occasional sentence. To recognize the man you live with. To feel the sun on your face and know it's the sun. To dance in place and know you are dancing.

Saturday's breakfast is a mix of two granola-type cereals topped with sliced banana, strawberries and raspberries, a peach, and some wild blueberries. The milk rises as I pour it in, and in a moment the berries are flooded with it. I bring her the full bowl and her half cup of coffee. Is there relief in her face, her bowels now emptied? No doubt, there's relief in mine.

Sunday

Catching up with music, I pop in a little Björk, but that doesn't seem to move her. Too early? Then it's Brubeck, old school, and that's followed by the *Pina* sound track, almost Latin like Charlie Byrd's *Corcovado*, and she lifts her elbows from the table, wobbling her coffee cup, and begins her seated dancing, eyes raised to the ceiling, lips parted in a half, transported smile. Then she's humming almost silently, and Sunday morning begins.

In winter, the old part of the house is closed off. No insulation or heat. That's where the sound system is, and we've been without music for many months, so I ordered a new Bose CD player. It sits atop the refrigerator, and the sound is of a good quality.

How long has it been since we went dancing? Neither of us were very good at it. But we were able to groove into each other's awkwardness. Dirty dancing at my niece's wedding reception, my mother looking on, a mix of pleasure and disapproval on her face. Music of this kind, jazz played for dancing, always brings back memory and is loved for that reason. A dark club near the university in Chicago when I was in high school. Even my clumsy fake ID was sufficient. James Moody, *Moody's Mood For Love*. Later it was California and King Pleasure. For Miriam it was political folk music, singing and guitars, Woody Guthrie and Pete Seeger. Social Work. Later, on this CD player, it's Chet Baker, Jim Hall and Paul Desmond, *Concierto de Aranjuez*. Miriam continues swaying, and I remember the mood of our lovemaking, as awkward and intimate as our dancing, Miles Davis on the turn table. Quiet Nights.

How far we have come and how variously. It was Roland Kirk who got me across the country, from L.A., through Aspen, into New York City. Miriam was recently back home from London and her Fulbright. We met on the occasion of a friend's play. Love at first sight? Not hardly, but a certain attitude that felt like romance was possible. People in New York hugged and kissed each other, even strangers, but I didn't touch her. It was that smile that got me, the same one that's on her lips this morning, dancing.

Now it's Gary Burton and Chick Corea and *Crystal Silence*, a little austerity to go with Miriam's cereal. She has the small circular container in her hands. *Little little little.* Jane brought it as a gift, immediately ignored, then in a week taken up. It's a nested box, two other's of graduated size inside, each one encrusted with blinking jewels. There's a mirror on the bottom, and Miriam gazes at herself in it, then turns it, curious, in her hands. She never opens it, and I'm tempted to say it's like her now, boxes within boxes, each one closed and sealed off from the others and from this surface I commune with, yet can't always understand. *God Bless the Child*, many versions on many disks. Now it's at least music that gets to her, every tune in the world made for dancing, as we did in the living room in Philadelphia on many occasions. Regardless of waltz tempo or foxtrot, we did our own thing as we used to say, and that thing was holding each other close, swaying. I'd kiss her on the neck or cheek, and we'd turn, part, and turn again, and again.

And this morning I'm her mother. "My mother," she says across the table. It seems at first absurd, but then

I see the way that I'm sitting, poised like her mother on the edge of my chair, ready always to rise up to assist her. Her mother would get more food, more drink, a tissue to wipe her nose or dry her tears. "Yes, I'm your mother," I say. And she smiles that smile, and I imagine her wink. Then it's *Embraceable You.*

a burden

I know a woman who had been married for fifty-three years, and yet she was only seventy when her husband died or passed away or went to a place called Heaven or some other paradise. The name doesn't matter, but that the woman spoke of his going as dying in what seemed a no nonsense way. Fifty-three years, married when he was nineteen, she seventeen, and pregnant. She was Irish, he of French heritage. They lived in a town beyond Boston, no more than a village when they were young. You might call them middle-class, but that would be an insufficient term to characterize residents of Foxboro.

And this woman had a dog, a toy poodle. She'd had it for almost eighteen years, and it had outlasted both her marriage and her husband. It was the only dog she'd ever owned or lived with or shared time with in her entire life, and the closeness between them, that solitary relationship, was not all that different from the one she'd had with her husband, her only lover, until I came along, at least in a dream, to possess her.

The dog was old and had grown ill, half-blind and incontinent, and this at a time when she was in deep and lasting mourning for the loss of her husband. He had made life easy for her, had taken care of her, and she missed him and his protective kindness profoundly.

Now she took care of her dog, most probably did so for too long a time, for the dog had done nothing for her, but to love her. Yet she could not face a second departure, so hard upon the first and more important one, and she knew the dog's death, which would be, unlike her husband's, a matter of choice, *her* choice, would be an increase in the weight of her mourning, the two deaths merging into something she thought might be unbearable.

Then she made her decision, and she told no one about it since it was a very private thing. She would have the dog put down. She didn't like the phrase. She would have him put to sleep. So she drove to a veterinarian she had dealt with before, the dog in his carrying case on the seat beside her. And the veterinarian was as kind as her husband would have been in this situation. She asked him if she might sit alone with the dog once he'd injected him, and he allowed this, keeping the room clear of any intrusion while she sat on a stool beside the surgical table. The dog licked her fingers, then his eyes closed and he sighed and was silent. She prayed for a moment over him, and when the veterinarian entered the room, she asked him, "Is he dead now?" The vet answered her in the affirmative and, noticing she was at loose ends, asked her to step out of the room for a few moments. And when he called her back in there was a small, sealed box on the table where the dog had rested.

"You can bury him in this," he said. And the woman thanked him and took the box in her arms. She went out to her car then and headed home, to where she had planned for the burial, asking a neighbor to dig a deep hole while she was away. And he had done so, and she placed the box in it and shoveled in the dirt and placed a stone owl and a few colorful rocks in the fresh turned soil as markers. Then she went into her empty house and wept.

I forgot to mention that this woman was very athletic. She was beautiful and had the body of a much younger woman, though given her age she had acquired a few ailments, a compromised knee that kept her from running, though she walked many miles each day at a strenuous pace, and a delicate back. And I forgot to mention too that once her husband was absent her dog grew more and more dependent upon her, somewhat annoyingly so, and that she had taken for the last year to carrying the dog in a backpack while she was working around the house and, most especially, preparing food or washing dishes in the kitchen.

She once said to me, "You know, I believe carrying my dog around this way has strengthened my back muscles." At least, I think I remember her saying this, and it seems to me that once the dog was gone and she was slightly stooped because of a deep though subtle depression brought on by the death of her husband, she commented on the fact that her back no longer seemed strong enough even for the brisk walking and the strenuous Pilates she worked through most mornings. She had plenty of heart for these things, but her strength, or maybe it was her will, was flagging.

She decided then that she must do something. So she went upstairs and got her husband's ashes. They were in a tightly woven bag, in a drawer, in her guest bedroom. And she went out into her yard and searched out a number of stones of different sizes and weights, and she brought these and the ashes into the bathroom and proceeded to weigh them on her scale, selecting various stones to rest beside the bag. Finally she had the weight as close to correct as she could get it, and she loaded the ashes and stones into her backpack and settled the pack on her shoulders. It felt just right. The ashes and the stones equaled the weight of her dog when she had carried him.

Now one can imagine this woman as she moves through her kitchen, preparing vegetables and various meats and poultry, then cooking them. The most domestic of tasks, though cooking for one can lose much in the way of enthusiasm as one thinks of that time when she will sit alone, no one across the table to pass things or to talk with. The woman carries the burden of her gone past on her back, a burden alive both in memory and in this case on her body as weight. But this weight does not pull her down, though memory might. As she moves from place to place, she begins to acquire a thing one might call backbone. Bearing the literal weight of her dead husband and the symbolic weight in cold stone of her dead dog, she has acquired a kind of grit that both acknowledges loss and puts it behind her. She is alone with this weight. It is a weight that puts my own difficulties into perspective. I am not alone. Though I'm engaged with someone, my Miriam, who is gradually leaving me here, I am not yet alone. How then can I not admire this woman and weep for her? How can I not love her?

standing above women

Here, in anticipation of a sad story, or two, or more. It's my first spring, after my first winter, here on Cape Cod. Saturday, and fields of buds on the wild blueberries, there also in anticipation, but of a richer harvest. Spring, then, and I imagine Miriam awaits my attention, sleeping peacefully, no thinking, but that's only my wish for peace. Empty of dreaming. It's raining, and I remember the sadness of the story my sister told me, the details forgotten because of my preoccupation with myself, my ego, and my own problems. Still, I remember enough of it, my grandmother's death, my sister and her husband absent. And that after tending to her and their six children for many years. A daughter, Becky, cutting a lock of her hair, my mother hysterical, peace of my grandmother without breath. My sister, after all those years, missing these events. My mother had left the room. Sue was playing the piano sweetly, and my mother went out to praise her. We all die alone. I have seen this, in cancer wards, in morgues, my brother, Jack, and I out for a cigarette, then returning to my mother's bedside. "She's gone," I say, and then he is weeping. Alone. Miriam is just sleeping. Will she be aware of it? Will I be aware of it for her? Alone. It's certain, when the time comes, that I will be. The world turns. I have no romance for it. "My father. Who are you? There's something I want to tell you…" Then nothing. She points to her head: "I don't know who I am."

A few years ago, many years ago, about thirty-five of them (how the years go by!), I went to visit my grandmother. She was, as I've said, living at my sister's house then. She was ill with a form of cancer of the bone, and she would spend the rest of her days there. My sister is a saint. Six children in the house still as I remember and my sister's husband, also a saintly figure. Especially when it came to my grandmother. We all, in fact, loved her. A very special person, as some grandmothers can be. Perhaps because they are well beyond the turmoil of children, that madness and responsibility and have hence come into the relaxation of maturity. Alvina, an old world name, but she was a modern woman in her spirit, though she had lost her husband at twenty-one, then her second husband, John when he was sixty in nineteen-fifty-nine, and then her only son, my father, when he was forty-three. Why is it the ones I love most must die, and why don't I? These words taken from a poem, never completed.

In the evening in my grandmother's kitchen in the town of Lyons, Illinois, I imagine in a spring many years ago, we would find ourselves sitting twilight, a term none of us was aware of. It was my grandmother's way, to let evening "steal" into the room. Steal, for though the darkness began with what seemed stationary shadows, their dissolution was so gradual and unmarked as to go unnoticed. It was our voices, slowly disembodied. Our vaguely seen faces, the lowered tones, as if we were in some sacristy, perhaps the slow drip of a faucet. Quiet words then, of the past and newly treasured moments in the nearer present. My grandmother, so matter of fact and exact, just church going and friends, coffee cake and hand dipped ice cream come summer, Mabel Milke across the street, Aunt Edna in her apartment up above.

Miriam is sleeping, perhaps dreaming. And so I stood there, above my grandmother, at her bed side, in my sister's house. The room had been an office or utility space of some kind. It was a pass through room, on the way to the garage. A small room, but it had been spruced up for her, flowers and colorful fabrics and subtle light. And she was thin and feeble where she lay, curled up on her side, yet smiling up at me. So what could I do but peel my clothing away, all but my undershorts, and climb into bed with her and make a spoon of my body, a place for her to sit. I held her very close then, close enough to hear her murmur: "Oh, Toby, Toby, Toby."

It is the same now with Miriam, in the early morning while she is still sleeping, perhaps fitfully. I stand above her, gaze down to attend her breathing in her back, examine her face, in repose, fear, or desperation, depending on the day and her possible dreams. I have tried to enter into her current reality, from time to time, in the way that I did with my grandmother on that day just months before she died. That time in bed with her was the last time that I touched her. But in the bed with Miriam, pressing against her, she grows rigid, confused by my presence or unable for some reason to respond. At first this hurt me. It still hurts me. And yet, in a while I find that all the hurts become conventional.

I have in my life stood above many women, in hospital wards and in surgeries, in medical clinics, on beaches, in motel rooms, in a field under a sky full of stars. And to be honest, though there are those who would find this insult, I see now that I had wanted to crawl into bed with all of them, to hold them close, to tell them of my love, possibly to make love to their frail bodies, careful of tubes and hanging bags, diapers and oxygen tanks. I know this is not conventional desire, and certainly I would not speak of it to others, fearing their disgust and disapproval.

So it goes, kind reader.

a life

When I was in Jail, only a brief stay brought on by adolescent rage at my father leaving me for death when I was seventeen, I asked my mother to bring me *The Amboy Dukes*, a book I'd been reading at the time of my incarceration. She brought me the Bible instead, thinking, I suppose, that it might help to cure me.

My mother was not very religious, at least not in a Bible sense, nor was Miriam's mother for that matter. For both of them, it seems to me, religion was more a matter of family tradition and old world influence than any form of theology. Faith played its part, but it was not much more than faith in the faith of those who had gone before them in belief. But my mother had brought me the Bible, and though I felt some anger that she had not brought the *Dukes*, I saw a look of bewilderment in her eyes, and not faith, as she handed the sacred text through the bars. Her visit ended quickly. That's the way it was in Jail.

So I read that book, and reading it led, in time, to my first novel, *The Life of Jesus*, a book I hoped to save from blasphemy through the use of a sub-title that named it apocryphal.

In the Old Testament, which she included with the New, there's plenty of violence brought on by people who seemed to bear no resemblance to the boy I was then. Everyone was an adult, even the children and animals. I cared nothing for them, and those pages, though unsettling, only reminded me of where I was and why I was there, and I didn't want to think about all that.

Then I came to Jesus. Well, came upon him that is, and being a troubled child I recognized that he did not conform to the Catechism, that interpretive document that I had been guided to read earlier, when I was a good-boy member of the church he had supposedly founded, that Catholicism that I was brought up in. He was no founder, he was a Jew, not a Catholic, how could he be, and was taken up as a figurehead by men who had named their organization after him. These are of course only the thoughts of a half-mad teenager in Jail.

   He was a wanderer and a loaner. He had an inner life, one that, because of his divinity, separated him from others. Nobody really knew him, not even his mother I thought, nor his father. He didn't have a dog, though I gave him one in my novel, nor were his friends, those apostles, really friends, but only followers. And when it came to sex in love, that power was notable, since it was never mentioned. So he was a model, what they call a role model these days, for me and, I suppose now, many other boys my age. The Church asked us, commanded us, to be like him, but not really like him. Not this solitary figure, this mysterious and disconnected man I had not been following, but had been walking beside. And I write of this only because, even at seventy-five, I have not changed.

   Here's a kind of miracle. If in the last days of our time together, I remember anything, one of things will be the time we first came to examine this house we'd purchased with great trepidation forty-three years ago. We had little money, and a mortgage seemed a frightening burden, though we went ahead with it.

We'd come up to Truro in April from New York City, and most of the stores near by were closed. We knew nothing of the neighboring towns then, and we'd made no plans for dinner. We examined the house thoroughly, making note of work to be done, cleaning chores, and possibilities for construction. A shed might be a study, a deck might be added. I might tear down a wall to make a larger bedroom out of the three smaller ones. Late afternoon. We'd cleaned and prepared a bed, hung towels in the small bathroom, turned the water on, checked that the stove was working. Then we were finished and hungry and at a loss to figure where we might find food. Here comes the miracle.

Our neighbor across the road, Donna Prada, who we had only just met, knocked at the door, and when we opened it, there she stood with a pheasant hanging down from her elevated hand. A pheasant! "Something for dinner?" she said, and after we thanked her profusely, no doubt wonder in our eyes, she was gone, and we considered the bird and what to do with it.

So I filled a bucket with hot water and placed it in the grass beside the porch. And Miriam dipped the pheasant into it and then worked to pull the feathers away. She was smiling of course, both at me and the bird, and once I'd gutted and washed it, she roasted the pheasant in our new oven, which was a very old oven, and in a while we sat down to our glorious dinner. We had no wine, but it was no matter. We toasted each other with cold well water. A formal dinner, of pheasant only. It was delicate, though gamey, and delicious. What more can one ask of life?

Other times and other memories, Miriam's favorite lamb chops, Wellfleet oysters, *Foie gras* outside of Paris, *Roesti* in Switzerland, wild rice harvested by Indians near my uncle's lake in Minnesota, a root beer float in Bisbee. This is not about food. These are fading beacons in the past, some of the ones that organize it. All gone now, but I can still taste them. Can Miriam? At dinner, a confused stir-fry that I had toiled over, she's trying to eat with the wrong end of her spoon. I point this out, and she nods and smiles, a twinkle in her eye, and turns it around. I laugh, and she laughs, at herself then, and digs in again. A *little little little* joke. We both get it. A rare occasion. I turn away and am quietly weeping.

Jesus was tempted but overcame temptation. I didn't. I was tempted by food, by women, by cigarettes, and in many cases gave in. I was tempted to pray, but only came to wishing. For the peace of conformity, of oblivion. I've lost weight, almost forty pounds in the last year. Miriam is almost skeletal. Were we to rise up at the end, we'd be lighter, though not like a feather. We're still weighted down by the past. At least I am.

Am I falling apart? I don't think so. It's Miriam, strange as it might seem, who keeps me together, though she doesn't know it. These daily tasks, all of which devolve to her body. Cleaning and washing, her face and hands and those other parts, touching her ribs and knees, brushing her hair. We are closer together in body than we have ever been. None of these moments is stored up in memory. Here we are. Here we will always be.

nasty Jack

My story, for the most part, is boring, told many times in the lives of others. Those early years. A typical childhood, marked by a little love and sibling rivalry, then adolescence, filled to the brim with disillusionment and strife. But I am not bored now. Out the window I see a gold finch at the feeder, a towhee taking a bath. A turkey pecks in the grass, head bobbing in the way of those wooden birds that dip down into a glass of water incessantly. Miriam is sleeping, and all the rest of the world in this neighborhood is waking up but me. I've been sitting here, looking out the window since three, seeing at first my dimly reflected face, then, coming on gradually, light of the dawning morning. Everything seems so lively and yet peaceful at the same time.

In the early summer in nineteen-fifty-two, I headed south of the border, to a town named Naco, hoping to lose my virginity, and that's what happened at a place of fascination and ill repute called The White House. There's nothing more to be said of that. Then, near the same time, I quit high school in my sophomore year and headed to California, which was a returning, and worked the night shift for a few months as an under-aged dish washer. There was nowhere to bed down, so I went back to Bisbee in time to leave again, this time to Illinois, to live with my uncle and aunt, sleeping in a chair that folded out into a bed. They are both dead now. No surprise, given my age and what theirs would be.

There's more of course, but I tire of memory and its attendant revisions, as if the past were actually there to be revised, then cherished and reentered. Fish swim, and birds gotta fly, but people must find their way beyond any dictations of nature. It was beautiful outside at three a.m., a light cool breeze, but for the bats racing through the dark sky like junk cars at a demolition derby. How easy the simile, without consequence. No stars, but the first summer full moon was up there. I went to bed in spring, Miriam beside me, but spring's gone now.

At Disneyland in Anaheim, there were Kodak Picture Sights. That's what the signs said. I know because I took photographs of them. And the scenes in question were already framed for the camera. If you aimed carefully, your photo looked like a postcard. Some things to store away, but for what reasons? Today, the term is gathering memories, saving them for some future. Wedding pictures, graduations, grave side caskets with family members in a row behind them (at least in Norway), any old thing at all, and birthdays. On my own birthdays, for many years, there were pictures of my special dinners. I'm sitting there with the food and my various presents gathered around me. There's saved up memories for you: my momentarily happy face, weight loss and gain, aging. It could have been Miriam behind the camera, and looking at these scenes I wish I could see her there. Those would be the photographs I might treasure.

Sometimes, in the summers when a child, there would be trips to exotic places, Knotts Berry Farm, Forest Lawn Cemetery, Magnum's Chinese Restaurant on Sunset Boulevard. Miriam and I did a little better at travel, though not often. I was a homebody, she wasn't, but my inertia won out. Now I wish I'd taken her to the places she desired. I had a chance to spend a semester teaching in Tokyo, but didn't take it. And Barcelona to see the Gaudís, a barge trip on the Seine, heading down to Rio. All these years and very few memories to speak of, but for those private ones that seem to be fading away. I could re-imagine them, like repurposing a piece of furniture, if I had time and inclination.

My first summer in Truro, I built a darkroom in the basement, then heard birds singing in the bright sun and wondered what I was doing there, in the dark, fussing with papers and chemicals, and I closed it down. Photographs are very much like death, all vital motion stopped, and that comes soon enough. Miriam is still sleeping, curled up, but she's breathing.

After pumping gas at Clark's Super 100, working in metallurgy at Reynolds Aluminum, loading boxcars for the CB and Q, I quit the suburbs of Chicago and headed west with John Culpepper, a casual friend, to California, yet another returning, searching I suppose for evidence of my dead father, places where he might have sat or looked out at a part of the world from, as if from one of those Kodak picture sights.

The trip itself was uneventful, but for the hitch-hiking soldier we picked up somewhere in Kansas I think, who turned out to be a magician. We stopped at some sights, made a side trip to Carlsbad Caverns, visited with a high-school girlfriend of mine, somewhere in Texas. There are photographs of much of this business, but not one depicts anything of interest in the background. It's just the three of us, pretending to be happy. Perhaps the soldier was. He had a ride after all.

Now I come to what might seem the darker part, at least for those who watch abbreviated autobiographies unfold on television. For all life stories must include tragedies, or at least difficulties, though these were no hard times for me, but rather revelatory as I see them now. And this will lead eventually to Miriam and our time together over the past ten or more years.

I joined the Navy. There was nothing else to do. I had no job, my car had broken down, John Culpepper had traveled back to Illinois and his family, and I was alone in California without prospects. It was nineteen-fifty-eight, between Korea and Vietnam, peace time, and I found myself in boot camp, marching across bridges break-step, so we would not, in the great power of our uniform stomping, bring them down. And after that, shaved heads, calisthenics, learning the parts of the M-1, I opted for what was available, clerical, dental or hospital corps school. I chose the last, and spent a few weeks doing nothing, awaiting the arrival of enough sailors to begin classes.

I was soon to be twenty-one, and on a day on which we were gathered together on the lawn outside the barracks for assignments and the Chief called out jobs that we might choose from, when work in the hospital morgue was mentioned my hand shot up for no reason I could understand then, but am somewhat clear about now.

The morgue. The night shift. Many people die in the night, and it was a large hospital, Balboa Naval Hospital in San Diego, and it was my job to receive the corpses, tag, check them in, and store there bodies until autopsy. And there were many autopsies in those few weeks, and while I was a little queasy in anticipation of them, half way into the first one only an intense interest remained.

There's a kind of good fellowship that arises between people who work together in the night while all others are sleeping, and the doctors were kind to me. And as I assisted, held retractors and weighed organs, I was privy to everything. These were victims of diseases and accidents that had killed them, and the doctors taught me the reasons for their deaths. I could see these reasons. Internal puncture wounds, calcified heart valves, bloated livers. I knew nothing of the meaning of life, but I saw the meaning of death, and though these people were beyond comfort or saving, that possibility came upon me in short order.

After the morgue and Hospital Corps School, I chose work on a cancer ward, ear, nose and throat, and after a quick orientation in the hands of a doctor and nurse, I was assigned to another corpsman in order to be introduced to the patient population. I thought of him then as a son-of-a-bitch, but now I see that he was only a crude and immature fool. I was a little older than he, but no less naive.

And this boy, for that's what he was, guided me to a curtained off bed at the end of the open ward. "Let me introduce you to Nasty Jack," he said, as he pulled the curtain away. And there, covered to the chest with a thin sheet, was a wasting-away man, I thought it was a man, whose bloated and unrecognizable as human face was hanging with chunks of suppurating flesh, his chest running with thick fluids and blood. He was sitting up, his head hanging down between his legs. It was the size of a small pumpkin, out of all proportion to his skeletal body. There was the strong, sickening scent of Air Wick in his makeshift cubicle. The boy laughed. "Hi Jack. This is Toby Olson. He's assigned to you now."

I was back in California, four years since my father's death. His decline had started in earnest here, and I see now seriously, even in its banality, that those few months spent tending to Jack were not so much an attempt to cure my father in imagination, but were a way to provide solace of a kind that had been impossible between my father and the son I was back then. I had been a child, perhaps I was still a child, but I was becoming a kind of professional when it came to the human body, and here I could do something. And I came to love Jack as I'd loved my father, and this was a pleasure to me and in some way fulfilling.

Jack couldn't talk, though the cancer hadn't at yet reached his vocal cords. But the swelling in his face and neck had squeezed and closed them down. He would gesture, wave his hands and turn his head, searching for my voice. His eyes were swollen shut, and he couldn't see, but sitting up, his head down, seemed to relieve some of his pain, and this is why he took up that posture, and that only increased the swelling. They had him in restraints, presumably so he wouldn't fall out of bed, but I could see that was not at issue, and I removed them. I remember he rubbed his wrists and seemed to look up in my direction in a gesture of what might have been thanks.

I washed his body, which had become filthy from lack of attention. And I provided him with a clean hospital gown, open at the front, so he could push it aside when the San Diego heat became oppressive and there was no breeze at the wide open windows. Though he was fed through a tube, I brought him cold ice cream and spread a towel under his chin, as a bib to catch the drops when I pressed the spoon into his swollen lips. I pressed towels against his face and neck to sop up the wet gunk that fell from his suppurating wounds, and each time I entered his cubicle, which was often, I urged him to lie back, lie back, so that the swelling would drain down into his body. I explained this to him. We could work together to accomplish this goal. In the end, though he'd have pain now, when the swelling was gone, he'd feel better. And I talked to him, about his time in the Navy, his family, and anything else I could think of, and though it was a one way conversation, I tried to make it conventional, just two sailors, one young and inexperienced, the other a wise senior. He'd nod and cock his head as if he might be smiling at my questions and comments, and I think he knew I cared for him, as no others on that ward had cared, that I saw value in him, and that maybe I was his friend. I became very efficient at this task, caring for the sick and dying, just as I have become efficient in caring for Miriam.

So Jack began to slowly recover his features. After a few weeks, his eyes opened and he could see me. Then in a while, the swelling in his lips receded, he could both see me and smile at me, and when the doctor came in for rounds, I suggested shyly that he might now be able to bandage Jack's throat and neck, and this was done. Jack lay back in his bed then, his wounds no longer visible, eyes open and alert. As his illness had progressed, morphine was now necessary, and he could sleep without nightmare.

Then one morning when I arrived on the ward, the curtains surrounding Jack's bed were gone, and where I had sat and talked to him, his wife and daughter now rested. They'd brought magazines and cookies and bits of clothing, and the three were in light conversation as I approached. Jack saw me, and he held up a magazine to give to me. "This is my friend, Toby," he said to his wife and daughter. Then he smiled and asked me if I'd like a cookie. I sat with them, and we talked for a while.

The next morning, Jack and his wife and daughter and the curtains and even the bed were gone. Jack had died in the night, and a week later I received a card of thanks from his wife. I think I gave him a little solace in his last days, and I still feel good about that. This had been no dark time for me.

Nor is there darkness as I care for Miriam. She is not like Jack or my father, though her leaving too is gradual and can be seen in her body. My father moved from a cane to crutches to a wheelchair and then bed, a narrow single in my grandmother's house, in which he died. Miriam can't walk without support. She moves about in a wheelchair most of the time, and, like Jack, she wears an adult bib when I feed her.

This house is not a hospital, nor is it much of a home anymore. And though the views from all the windows remain essentially the same, it seems to have shifted a bit on its axis, and it's up to me to keep it from spinning out of control, to keep myself from doing that. Most everything medically needed is close at hand, pills and mineral oil, peroneal fluid, suppositories and enema bags, even drugs for eventual pain down in the refrigerator. But there is nothing here for curing, just some things that might keep a fading life bearable. And I often feel as if I'm that hospital corpsman again, though much older now, there only for support and whispered kindness. I know I've repeated myself, but that's because our life together is mostly routine, and the problem with routine is that it becomes mechanical, and I must guard against that, lest I too become a machine and lose her before she's gone. When it's only anger or despair that brings me back to her in this present, I'm in trouble and so is she. So I count on moments of surprise, and though they are few -a hint of humor, a complete sentence, "My Mother," a smile when I touch her anus- they hold me to a focus that I dare not lose. Let it continue then, dear Miriam, surprise, music, and of course dancing, until it can't.

the other woman

The world's at peace this morning, at least this fraction of it is. Who knows what happens elsewhere. I've not read the New York Times on line in days, but here the breeze has died down completely and though overcast, there is no promise of rain. A promise? What kind of language is that? Forecasters at a loss for words. But looking back to yesterday and then ahead to tomorrow, there's rain and wind. Been there, coming yet again. Here green leaves are almost stationary on the branches, only the second hand is moving, and in the distance, beyond those trees that need some trimming, the bay is a crystal silence, yet again some music as metaphor.

Every day, every hour through early autumn's variety, the past comes back to distract me. This is why I forget things, tasks in the immediate, the shallow steepness of the stairs, this, and some low level anxiety that keeps me moving, often without thought for the present.

Last week I drove to the cemetery, Pine Grove, to examine our plots. They're the size of a double bed, Miriam on the left, I on the right, our bodies only in imagination, for we will find our peace in incineration, ashes in nondescript urns. Peace? That's a kind of language only. The ground is rough, but a handsome juniper will shade us. Yet who will come to stand above and imagine us, side by side, never moving or touching, in that bed together, but completely alone? An angel the size of the baby Jesus is carved on a child's stone a few feet away. We're down in an indentation, always looking up, but in reality we are only ashes. We could slip through fingers like sand. There will be a stone, carefully chosen, unless I leave first.

It's six-ten, and I've been smoking again, after almost ten years free of it. A Swiss friend came to be with us two weeks ago, smoking like a chimney, and it's then that I started. I have one cigarette left. That will be the last one. I said the same thing a week ago and then continued. Perhaps this time I'll be successful, as I seem to succeed with Miriam, day in and day out. I don't know why. When my friend and his wife left, the house seemed empty, and maybe it was that. The two of us alone in our own worlds, but for those times of unintentional touch and imagined communication that drifted up to the ceiling between us, like smoke rings. It is and it isn't a lost cause.

Fingerling potatoes over pasta in a pesto sauce, the basil homegrown on the front deck. That's dinner tonight. Salad and a glass of Pino Grigio for me. I do the best I can, though I am no cook. Miriam was. Beautiful celebratory dinners and fine deserts on my birthday in August for many years. This August I'll be seventy-six. No celebration. Sad sack. Soon I'll go in and get her up. That routine a kind of saving grace, a return from memory.

My friend Larry is reading the obituaries avidly, so many people dying in their seventies. He's a year older than I, and he speaks often of the little time he has left. I tell him he only needs to make it for a few more years. Then he'll be eighty and home free. It's a weak joke between us. Another friend, Nathaniel, called the other day. He's eighty-five now, and though he doesn't say it in words, he may be figuring the end is near. It's always near. He complains of a few ailments, but when he speaks of poetry, readings he's given, his sweet irony and enthusiasm is the same as always. Then there's Walt Rogers, my next door neighbor for thirty-five years. He's now in a nursing home down south. I call him on the phone most months and we talk science and politics. His mind's as sharp as the proverbial tack. He's ninety-seven and still interested. These old friends. I can make nothing of all this, but for a complexity of thought and feeling, which seems to me, at this moment at least, to be living.

There will be music later, something to get us started, and Miriam will be dancing in her seat. That's a sure thing. I count on it. Then, most probably, we'll be sitting out on the deck, under the umbrella, waiting for the Bobwhites, the return of the wild turkey. I'll be thinking about that and Miriam won't. It's the way of things now, anticipation and immediacy.

When I was a young boy, I couldn't sit still. I'd race from place to place until my mother stopped me. Exhausted and sweaty and still vibrating with unspecified enthusiasm. She'd sit me down and touch my hair and arms until I cooled off. I remember her posture, bending over above me, looking down at me. I remember her scent and bits of the recurring situations. Her scent is still vivid, the rest fractured and reformed in loss in memory.

All my life I have been lingering in the past, in a soupy nostalgia where I supposed things were better. My ill father on his feet again, my mother's cut hands from work at the factory healed, a fourth of July picnic where all of my dead relatives were healthy and alive again, and I was racing around holding a model airplane above my head. Illinois, California, Arizona, Texas, all these isolate nodes of experience that I have left behind. And I have written of this, the disillusionment of characters who have managed to go back, only to find nothing but more corrective memories in yet another past romance. This has been the music I've counted on, slow jazz tunes devoid of all dissonance. And the recognition of this warped way of living, in the writing at least, has led me to believe that to be really alive is to live in a perpetual present.

From the beginning and almost up to the present, and this fortified by attitudes of others in my Alzheimer's Care Givers Group, I've thought of Miriam's condition as a failing, yet another opportunity for me to look back to better times. I no longer think this way, for I now see that Miriam is the other woman and that she lives, always, right here.

Entering naked into the bathroom, or entering the kitchen, or turning her head to look up at me at bedside, there's often a look on her face that says Oh, I'm right here, what is this new place? Who is this man? Her eyes are focused, inquisitive and vibrantly alive. Right here, this place, her life. This is not my world, though it is surely hers.

And so we live together in these separate realities. There are moments of connection, but they are few. It is not so much loss as change that I see in her. Apart and together. I am still here. Miriam is still here. And this is not yet the end.

Miriam imagined

I awaken. Is this a dream? My father is standing above me. "My father." "Yes, I am your father," he says, "Your husband." What is this place? A chair. Light at the window. Now he pulls back the cover, rubs my legs and lifts them. I'm sitting at the edge. "Are you the other one?" I ask. "Yes," he says, "I'm me." I'm on my feet. He holds my hands. He's walking backward! Then he moves my arms. I'm dancing a *little little little little little little*. What is this room? A bathroom. He leads me to that place to pee and sits me down. Am I naked? "My mother?" I ask. He's smiling. "Yes, I am your mother." "There's something I want to tell you," I say. And then it's gone.

This is cereal. Fruit, banana, milk. I put my fingers in it and he lifts them out and wipes them and I put they back in. Is this a kitchen? Last night. Was it last night? Something. A dream? My mother, my father, my sisters. We were at a table. Someone was talking. Was it me? We were all, what is the word, happy? On Teller Avenue, in the Bronx, Manhattan, London, Aspen, Philadelphia, Truro. "Eat your cereal," he says, "with the spoon." In the dream we were all happy. There were things to talk about. Social Work? What is that all about? Case Western Reserve. Andy. Somebody else.

What day is this? Is this a day? This is Pat washing me. I don't like this water. Pat is nice to me. She's so beautiful. I love her. "You're beautiful," she says. Why is she whispering? Now she's rubbing my hair. Now she's brushing my hair. *Little little little*, something in my hand to show her. It's a glove. She gives it to me. I squeeze it. Now she's putting on my diaper. A diaper! It's disgusting. I don't wear such things. Then she's putting on my pants and then I'm riding down in a chair. I like it. This riding.

"Do you know who I am?" he asks me. No, I shake my head. "I'm your husband," he says, "We've been married for forty-six years." How shocking. "I don't know who I am," I say. "You're Miriam," he says. "Oh," I say, "But why am I here?" "This is home," he says. "Oh," I say.

These things are childish, this baby talking. "You're sooo sweet! You have a lovely smile!" Am I a baby? Shut up, you son-of-a-bitch. "Isn't she sweet!" As if I am not here. Where am I? "Here," he says. "In the living room." I'm in my chair. He calls it your chair. It rolls. Out big windows, birds float by. What is this place? Pictures on the wall. A leather couch. Another *leather leather leather* is a chair. "What is this place?" "Home," he says, "Your living room." "Oh," I say.

I believe I have been here before. I'm wearing a hat. I feel the sun on the side of my face. It's burning in. Perhaps it will be tomorrow, this time I am here. Perhaps yesterday. What is yesterday? There were fashionable women standing in a big circle at a party. They talk of cooking and children. I have no children, but I am a very good cook. There was a dish I made, or will make, or am making, on the biggest of occasions. I have forgotten what it was.

Now the women are dispersing, a little nervous I think, being among women only, and are searching out their husbands. Where are they? Do I have one? It doesn't matter. I am the cook, the Social Worker. What is that, a Social Worker? The women find their husbands and melt away into them. I'm in a very large hall. Many women and men. Somebody is at a podium, speaking. He's talking about me! What is this celebration? He's talking about me. He finishes, and another person arises and talks again about me. What have I done? Am I in trouble? Will I have to say something? I can't do that.

Now we are traveling someplace. I don't know where. I'll send her to the moon! To the moon! Somebody said that. I don't know how or when. I don't understand what I'm doing here. "We're going home," he says. "My father?" He laughs. "Yes, indeed, I am your father." "My father," I say. I have come from somewhere to get here. It is a dark place, yet a place nonetheless. And in this place, of shadows and whispers, I think there's a population, many speakers and gestures. I cannot see them, but were I able I believe they would provide, in their articulating bodies, points on a map of my past life, they would provide anchors to hold me in places in the memory. Fancy that. I don't know if I am dreaming here. "No," he says. "You're not dreaming. You're going home." "Didn't they serve lamb chops?" I say. "Yes," he says. "A mountain! Your favorite food."

Once, in a time when I was lucid, my husband, his name is Toby, bought me a bicycle, so that I could ride along beside him on the country roads of Truro. I knew from the start that I would never be riding. I was brought up only for roller skates, and even that activity was severely limited by my mother's anxiety.

It was my birthday, and Toby had strung a banner announcing it above the fireplace in our apartment in

New York City. He called out to me, using our special name, a name that is private and will not be revealed here. The bike sat on the brick hearth, ribbons woven into the spokes, sprays of them hanging down from the handlebar grips. I was both surprised and intimidated by it.

Summer is not for me, and once the brown-tail moth began to eat me, neither was gardening. Truro was our special retreat, but most of the specialness remained inside the house, in the car, marketing, listening to music, dancing in the living-room when the tune was right, and most of all visiting with friends and talking to strangers. My life has been a life of the mind and of feeling, but one always steered into action in the service of others, my husband, students, and those others who needed what little help I could manage to give them. I love these others, the poor in sustenance and the poor in mind and spirit, and I have tried always to salve the wounds of these others and to teach students the ways in which they might do the same. And I think I have been successful in my small way. I have loved these others and my time and life with them.

Now I'm another woman, and it falls upon Toby to take my place as giver, and even his awkwardness in this task has brought me some peace of mind. He has washed me, cleaned up after me, cooked for me, fed me and held my hands, and I have tried to tell him of my gratitude with my eyes and smiles. But I'm not sure he understands. Once, in a green haze of pollen, when he was wheeling me to the car, we saw a bold, red cardinal sitting on a bare branch. I remarked on it. I'd seen it and I remarked on it. He seemed delighted. "Yes!" he said,

"A bird!"

Comes a time now when I am not talking. I can talk. But I cannot say things. I start, "What do you think of…," then comes nothing. I will not talk. "What is this?" I say. "Your coffee cup," he says. "Be careful, the coffee's hot." I'm a *little little little little little little* careful. "I get that," he says. "Little little. Are you dancing there?" "Yesss," I say.

Believing in a life spent in momentary pleasure. Someone is saying that. Or something. I remember. The Gathering Place. Some are talking. Most are silent. Yet some are smiling. I'm smiling. Now I'm on a bus with big Barbara. She's holding her plastic baby. We are going somewhere, in the rain. I can't remember where we started. It must be late in the day, because I'm tired. Now the bus stops. Its side opens. A man comes and takes away my shackles. He turns my chair and wheels me to the ramp. And there is this other man on the ground outside. He's smiling up at me. Is it my father, Toby, or the other one? I don't know. "My father?" I say. "Yes," he says. "Welcome home."

Miriam Meltzer Olson
1933-2014